Kaua'i

IMAGES OF THE GARDEN ISLAND

Photography by

Douglas Peebles

Mutual Publishing

Library of Congress Catalog Card Number: 2004106193
ISBN-10: 1-56647-668-2
ISBN-13: 978-1-56647-668-3

Fifteenth Printing, February 2015

Mutual Publishing, LLC
1215 Center Street, Suite 210
Honolulu, Hawai'i 96816
Ph: (808) 732-1709 Fax: (808) 734-4094
Email: info@mutualpublishing.com
www.mutualpublishing.com
Printed in Taiwan

A hike through the Ohiʻa Forest uncovers sweeping views and small pleasures,
like an up-close glimpse of the famed lehua flower.

Waves break against lava rocks on the edge of Kauapea Beach on the shore.

Surf rushes up onto the sand near Kīlauea Point.

Just after sunset Hanalei Pier is framed by a dark rainbow sky.

A secluded view of Poʻipū Beach without the many cottages and condominiums that line its shore.

Furling clouds are set aflame by the setting sun.

Razor edge ridges reach into the clouds in Kalalau Valley.

The expanse of soaring cliffs on the Nāpali Coast plunge steeply into the sea.

Alaka'i Swamp is actually a dewy rainforest rising up from the Pacific.

High surf during the winter months carve new imprints into the shore of the rugged Nāpali Coast.

Towering coconut palms meet a near-cloudless sky in Wailua.

The delicate fronds of the taro plant stretch deep into the Kaua'i Refuge Complex.

Windswept palms tower above the changing blues of Kēʻē Beach.

The northernmost tip of Kīlauea National Wildlife Refuge is one of the few refuges open to the public.

The many layered cliffs of Waimea Canyon
hint at the natural history of this oldest main Hawaiian island.

The carved ridges of the Nāpali Coast rise 4,000 feet straight into the sky.

The majority of Hawai'i's taro, a staple of the Hawaiian diet, is grown in the Hanalei Valley Taro Field.

Hula dancers offer a story of Hawai'i's cultural heritage at Smith's Tropical Paradise.

Waterfalls slip through the crevices of this emerald mountainside.

Lumaha'i Beach was the stunning backdrop for the performance of
"I'm Gonna Wash That Man Right Out of My Hair" in the film *South Pacific*.

The sun sets in brilliant oranges and yellows over Hanalei Bay.

Kayakers traverse the winding Nāpali Coast by sea, camping along the way.

Kalalau Valley, seen from the lookout at Kōkeʻe, gives the dramatic picture of steepled peaks and knife-edged ridges.

Niʻihau can be seen across the ocean from the west side of the island on days when the skies are clear.

Rocks dotting the sand of Kalalau Beach seem to glow as the sun begins to fall behind the pali.

The terraced landscape of Limahuli Garden, Hā'ena.

Giant-sized lily pads float in the pond at Pacific Tropical Botanical Gardens.

Nicknamed "The Grand Canyon of the Pacific," Waimea Canyon is ten miles long, roughly a mile wide, and 3,600 feet deep.

Honopū Valley, one of the most remote valleys on Kauaʻi's spectacular Nāpali Coast.

The earthtones of Waimea Canyon's cliffs are due to vegetation
and soil that has eroded over millions of years.

The Nēnē Goose, here traversing Kalalau, is Hawai'i's endangered state bird.

Wailua Beach seen through the trunks and fronds
of coconut palm silhouettes on the south side of the Wailua River.

Kīpū Kai Valley, south of Nawiliwili Bay, is a private working cattle ranch.

West Kauaʻi Methodist Church solemnly sits in the middle of a sugarcane field.

A Hawaiian Monk Seal lazily snoozes and suns itself on Wailua beach.

Outrigger sailing canoe in Hanalei Bay.

The indigo waters of Hanakāpī'ai Beach can be seen in the distance from the Kalalau Trail.

Wailua Falls plunges eighty feet into the cool fresh water pool below.

A bird's eye view of the Nāpali Coast shows its dramatic cliffs and rugged shoreline.

Hawai'i's state flower, the hibiscus, grows in many color combinations.

Hanalei Bay with outrigger canoes onshore.

Spouting Horn near Poʻipū explodes as sea water splashes out of a shoreline lava tube.